I0018745

The Ethical Hacker's Handbook

A Practical Guide to Penetration Testing

By

Mark David

Table of contents

Introduction

Ethical hacking, also known as penetration testing or white-hat hacking, is a critical aspect of modern cybersecurity. With the ever-increasing prevalence of cyber threats, ethical hackers play a pivotal role in safeguarding systems, networks, and data from malicious actors. This introduction explores the role of ethical hackers, the legal and ethical frameworks governing their activities, and the skills and certifications required to excel in this domain.

The Role of Ethical Hackers in Cybersecurity

Ethical hackers are professionals authorized to identify and mitigate security vulnerabilities in an organization's digital infrastructure. They use the same tools and techniques as malicious hackers but with a constructive purpose: to protect rather than exploit.

1. Proactive Threat Identification:

Ethical hackers perform penetration tests to simulate cyberattacks, uncovering weaknesses before real attackers can exploit them. These tests are essential for ensuring the security of systems, applications, and networks.

2. Securing Sensitive Data:

Organizations rely on ethical hackers to safeguard sensitive information such as financial records, customer data, and intellectual property. A single breach can lead to catastrophic financial and reputational damage.

3. Compliance and Regulation:

Many industries, including finance, healthcare, and government, have strict cybersecurity regulations. Ethical hacking ensures compliance with standards like PCI-DSS, GDPR, HIPAA, and ISO 27001.

4. Incident Response Preparation:

Ethical hackers often work with incident response teams to test the robustness of an organization's defenses. This preparation enables quicker recovery in the event of a breach.

By identifying vulnerabilities, ethical hackers serve as the first line of defense in an organization's cybersecurity strategy, ensuring that security measures evolve to counter emerging threats.

Legal and Ethical Considerations

Ethical hacking operates within a framework of laws and ethical guidelines. Understanding these boundaries is essential to ensure that penetration testing activities remain lawful and responsible.

1. Legal Framework:

- Authorization: Ethical hacking must be conducted with explicit permission from the organization. Unauthorized activities, even if well-intentioned, can lead to legal consequences.

- Data Privacy Laws: Ethical hackers must adhere to data protection regulations, ensuring that sensitive data accessed during tests is not misused or exposed.

- Non-Disclosure Agreements (NDAs): These agreements protect organizations by ensuring that ethical hackers do not share confidential information.

2. Ethical Principles:

- Integrity: Ethical hackers must report all vulnerabilities discovered during testing, even if it reflects poorly on the organization.

- Transparency: Ethical hackers should communicate their methods and findings clearly and openly with stakeholders.

- Accountability: Ethical hackers are responsible for ensuring their actions do not unintentionally harm systems or data.

3. Consequences of Non-Compliance:

Violating legal or ethical guidelines can result in criminal charges, loss of professional credibility, and damage to the ethical hacking profession as a whole.

By adhering to these principles, ethical hackers maintain trust and legitimacy in their role as cybersecurity professionals.

Skills and Certifications

Becoming an effective ethical hacker requires a combination of technical expertise, analytical thinking, and a commitment to continuous learning.

Specific certifications also play a crucial role in demonstrating competency.

1. Core Skills:
- Networking Knowledge: Understanding network protocols, configurations, and topologies is fundamental to identifying vulnerabilities in connected systems.
- Operating Systems Expertise: Familiarity with Windows, Linux, and macOS systems is essential for penetration testing.
- Programming and Scripting: Proficiency in languages like Python, JavaScript, and Bash enables ethical hackers to create custom scripts and tools.
- Problem-Solving and Creativity: Ethical hackers must think like attackers, finding innovative ways to bypass defenses.

2. Popular Certifications:

- Certified Ethical Hacker (CEH): A widely recognized certification that provides foundational knowledge of penetration testing tools and techniques.
    - Offensive Security Certified Professional (OSCP): Known for its hands-on exam, the OSCP certification is highly respected among professionals seeking advanced penetration testing skills.
    - Certified Information Systems Security Professional (CISSP): While broader in scope, CISSP provides a strong foundation in security concepts relevant to ethical hacking.
    - CompTIA PenTest+: Focused on penetration testing and vulnerability management, this certification is ideal for beginners.
    - GIAC Penetration Tester (GPEN): A certification emphasizing practical skills and advanced penetration testing methodologies.

3. Continuous Learning:

Cybersecurity is a rapidly evolving field. Ethical hackers must stay updated on the latest threats, tools, and technologies by:
- Participating in hacking competitions and Capture the Flag (CTF) events.
 - Following cybersecurity blogs, forums, and podcasts.
- Engaging with the ethical hacking community on platforms like GitHub and LinkedIn.

Ethical hacking combines technical expertise with a deep sense of responsibility. By understanding their role, operating within legal and ethical frameworks, and continuously improving their skills, ethical hackers can significantly contribute to a safer digital world.

Chapter 1: Foundations of Ethical Hacking

Ethical hacking is a cornerstone of modern cybersecurity, providing the tools, techniques, and methodologies to safeguard systems and data. In this chapter, we delve into the fundamental concepts, types of hackers, and the structured approach used in ethical hacking.

Key Concepts

Understanding the foundational concepts of vulnerability, exploit, and payload is essential for ethical hackers. These terms form the basis of penetration testing and vulnerability assessment.

1. Vulnerability:

A vulnerability is a weakness or flaw in a system, application, or network that attackers can exploit. These flaws can arise from:

- Software Bugs: Errors in code that lead to security gaps.
- Configuration Issues: Misconfigured firewalls, permissions, or access controls.
- Human Factors: Social engineering vulnerabilities due to lack of awareness or training.

Ethical hackers identify these weaknesses to help organizations patch them before malicious actors can take advantage.

2. Exploit:

An exploit is a specific method or tool used to take advantage of a vulnerability. Exploits can be:

- Automated Scripts or Programs: Tools like Metasploit provide prebuilt exploits for testing.

- Custom Code: Written by attackers or ethical hackers to target specific vulnerabilities.

For instance, exploiting an SQL injection vulnerability can allow attackers to access unauthorized data from a database.

3. Payload:
A payload is the malicious code delivered through an exploit to execute a specific action. Payloads vary depending on the attacker's intent, such as:
- Reverse Shells: Grant attackers control over a target system.
- Data Exfiltration Tools: Steal sensitive information.
- Ransomware: Encrypt files and demand payment for decryption.

Ethical hackers simulate payload delivery to understand how attackers might operate, but without causing harm.

Hackers are categorized based on their intent and approach. Ethical hackers must understand these distinctions to navigate their role effectively.

1. Black Hat Hackers:
   - Intent: Malicious and illegal.
   - Goal: Steal data, disrupt services, or cause harm for personal, financial, or political gain.
   - Methods: Use sophisticated tools to exploit vulnerabilities without authorization.
   - Examples: Cybercriminals running ransomware campaigns or selling stolen data on the dark web.

2. White Hat Hackers:
   - Intent: Authorized and ethical.
   - Goal: Help organizations identify and fix vulnerabilities.

- Methods: Use the same tools as black hats but operate with permission and transparency.

- Examples: Ethical hackers performing penetration tests or bug bounty hunters reporting vulnerabilities.

3. Grey Hat Hackers:

- Intent: Ambiguous; neither fully ethical nor entirely malicious.

- Goal: Often act without permission but with no harmful intent, such as exposing security flaws publicly to pressure organizations into fixing them.

- Examples: Hackers who uncover vulnerabilities and post them online without informing the affected organization first.

Understanding these types helps ethical hackers maintain their professionalism and avoid crossing into unethical or illegal territory.

Ethical hacking follows a structured methodology to ensure thorough and legal testing. This process mirrors the steps malicious hackers take but is conducted with authorization and documentation.

1. Reconnaissance:
- Objective: Gather information about the target system or network.
- Techniques:
  - Passive Reconnaissance: Observing without interacting with the target (e.g., searching public records or social media).
  - Active Reconnaissance: Interacting with the target (e.g., ping sweeps, network scanning).
- Tools: Nmap, Wireshark, Shodan.

2. Scanning:
- Objective: Identify live systems, open ports, and potential vulnerabilities.

- Techniques:
    - Port Scanning: Identifying active ports using tools like Nmap.
    - Vulnerability Scanning: Assessing systems for known flaws using tools like Nessus or OpenVAS.

3. Gaining Access:
    - Objective: Exploit identified vulnerabilities to access the target system.
- Techniques:
    - Exploiting unpatched software.
        - Brute force attacks to crack passwords.
    - Tools: Metasploit, Hydra, John the Ripper.

4. Maintaining Access:
    - Objective: Ensure continuous access to the compromised system.
    - Techniques:
        - Installing backdoors.
        - Creating persistent user accounts.

- Ethical Consideration: Ethical hackers document methods without installing persistent threats.

5. Covering Tracks:

   - Objective (Malicious Hackers): Erase evidence of their activity.
   - Ethical Approach: Ethical hackers document the methods used but avoid tampering with logs.

6. Reporting:

   - Objective: Provide a comprehensive report of findings and recommendations.
   - Details:
   - Vulnerabilities discovered.
   - Steps taken during the test.
   - Suggested mitigations.

   Clear documentation ensures stakeholders understand the risks and can implement corrective actions.

The foundational knowledge of vulnerabilities, exploits, and payloads, coupled with an understanding of hacker types and the structured hacking methodology, equips ethical hackers with a roadmap for responsible and effective penetration testing. This framework not only mirrors the approach of malicious actors but also ensures ethical hackers stay within legal and professional boundaries, protecting systems while maintaining trust.

Chapter 2: Setting Up Your Environment

The foundation of effective ethical hacking lies in a well-configured environment. Before executing tests, ethical hackers must set up tools, platforms, and a controlled lab for experimentation and learning. This chapter delves into essential tools like Kali Linux, Metasploit, and Burp Suite, the process of creating a virtual lab, and the best practices to ensure a robust and secure setup.

Tools and Platforms

Ethical hackers rely on a variety of specialized tools and platforms to conduct penetration testing effectively. Among the most widely used are Kali Linux, Metasploit, and Burp Suite.

1. Kali Linux:

- Overview:

Kali Linux is a Debian-based distribution specifically designed for penetration testing and security assessments. It comes preloaded with hundreds of tools tailored for ethical hacking.

- Features:

- Comprehensive suite of tools for network scanning, vulnerability assessment, and exploitation.

- Lightweight and compatible with multiple platforms, including virtual machines and cloud environments.

- Regular updates to stay current with cybersecurity trends.

- Common Tools Within Kali:

- Nmap: Network scanning and discovery.

- Aircrack-ng: Wireless network penetration testing.

- John the Ripper: Password cracking.

- Wireshark: Network protocol analysis.

2. Metasploit Framework:
- Overview:

Metasploit is one of the most popular tools for developing, testing, and executing exploits. It provides a modular framework for ethical hackers to simulate real-world attacks.

- Features:

- Exploit modules for targeting vulnerabilities.

- Payloads to deliver and execute code on the target system.

- Auxiliary modules for tasks like scanning and fuzzing.

- Post-exploitation modules for privilege escalation and data collection.

- Use Case Example:

A hacker uses Metasploit to exploit a known vulnerability in a web server, gaining shell access to the system.

3. Burp Suite:
- Overview:

Burp Suite is a web vulnerability scanner and penetration testing toolkit designed for evaluating web application security.
- Features:
    - Intercepting Proxy: Captures and manipulates HTTP/HTTPS traffic between the browser and the server.
    - Scanner: Automated identification of vulnerabilities like SQL injection and cross-site scripting (XSS).
    - Intruder: Customizable tool for brute-forcing and parameter fuzzing.
- Use Case Example:
    Testing a web application for SQL injection vulnerabilities by intercepting and modifying HTTP requests.

These tools provide the functionality needed for comprehensive penetration testing and are essential in an ethical hacker's arsenal.

A virtual lab is a controlled environment where ethical hackers can practice skills, test exploits, and experiment without risking real-world systems.

1. Why Set Up a Virtual Lab?

- Provides a safe space to test tools and techniques.

- Prevents unintentional harm to production systems or networks.

- Enables replication of real-world scenarios for training and learning.

2. Components of a Virtual Lab:

- Host Machine: The physical computer or server hosting the virtual environment.

- Virtualization Software: Tools like VMware Workstation, VirtualBox, or Hyper-V to create and manage virtual machines (VMs).

- Operating Systems: A mix of targets, including Windows, Linux, and macOS, for testing.

- Vulnerable Applications: Pre-configured environments like Metasploitable, DVWA (Damn Vulnerable Web Application), or OWASP Juice Shop for hands-on practice.

3. Setting Up the Lab:
- Install virtualization software on the host machine.

- Download and configure VMs for tools like Kali Linux and target systems like Metasploitable.

- Network the virtual machines to simulate real-world connectivity.

- Secure the lab by isolating it from external networks to prevent unintended breaches.

4. Testing Scenarios:
- Simulate phishing attacks within the lab.

- Practice exploiting vulnerabilities in web applications.

- Experiment with privilege escalation techniques on target VMs.

Best Practices for Ethical Hacking Setups

To ensure an efficient and secure ethical hacking environment, follow these best practices:

1.   Isolate   Your   Testing Environment:
- Always isolate your virtual lab from your main network to avoid accidental breaches or data leaks.
- Use network segmentation or an air-gapped setup for additional security.

2. Keep Tools Updated:
- Regularly update tools like Kali Linux, Metasploit, and Burp Suite to access the latest features and vulnerability databases.
- Monitor updates from the developers' official channels.

3. Document Your Work:

- Maintain detailed records of your testing environment, configurations, and findings.

- Use note-taking tools like CherryTree or Joplin to organize observations and results.

4. Respect Legal and Ethical Boundaries:

- Only test on systems and networks for which you have explicit permission.

- Avoid experimenting on live production environments unless explicitly authorized.

5. Back Up Your Environment:

- Regularly back up your virtual machines and configurations to prevent data loss due to hardware failure or errors.

- Use snapshot features in virtualization software to save and restore states.

6. Practice Good Cyber Hygiene:

- Secure your tools and platforms with strong passwords and encryption.
- Regularly scan your lab environment for vulnerabilities to prevent self-inflicted issues.

7. Leverage Community Resources:

- Participate in forums like Reddit, Hack The Box, or Bugcrowd for troubleshooting and knowledge sharing.
- Use CTF platforms like TryHackMe or VulnHub to practice in structured scenarios.

Setting up the right environment is a critical first step in ethical hacking. Tools like Kali Linux, Metasploit, and Burp Suite provide the necessary capabilities, while a virtual lab offers a secure and controlled space for testing. By adhering to best practices, ethical hackers can ensure their setups are efficient, safe, and aligned with professional standards. This preparation not only enhances skill development but also lays the groundwork for successful and responsible penetration testing.

Chapter 3: Reconnaissance and Information Gathering

Reconnaissance, often the first step in ethical hacking, involves collecting information about a target to identify potential vulnerabilities. This process lays the groundwork for subsequent stages of penetration testing. By thoroughly understanding the target, ethical hackers can create effective attack strategies while ensuring their methods remain ethical and authorized.

Passive vs. Active Reconnaissance

Reconnaissance can be divided into two main categories: passive and active. Each approach has distinct methods and tools, serving different purposes in the information-gathering process.

1. Passive Reconnaissance:

- Definition: Collecting information about a target without directly interacting with it. This method minimizes the risk of detection.
- Techniques:
- WHOIS Lookup: Retrieving domain registration details, including the registrant's name, organization, and contact information.
- Social Media Analysis: Monitoring a target's social media accounts for personal or corporate insights.
- DNS Enumeration: Identifying subdomains and email servers using tools like nslookup and Dig.
- Advantages:
- Low risk of detection.
- Provides valuable insights without alerting the target.
- Limitations:
- Restricted to publicly available information.
- May not uncover technical vulnerabilities.

2. Active Reconnaissance:

- Definition: Directly interacting with the target to gather detailed information. This approach carries a higher risk of detection.
- Techniques:
    - Port Scanning: Identifying open ports on a target system using tools like Nmap.
    - Ping Sweeps: Determining live hosts on a network.
    - Banner Grabbing: Extracting service information from open ports to identify running software and versions.
- Advantages:
    - Provides detailed and actionable insights.
    - Identifies specific vulnerabilities and attack vectors.
- Limitations:
    - Higher risk of being detected by intrusion detection systems (IDS).
    - May raise legal or ethical concerns without proper authorization.

Ethical hackers must decide on the appropriate approach based on the scope of their engagement and the rules of engagement (RoE) agreed upon with their clients.

Tools for Reconnaissance and Information Gathering

Ethical hackers use various tools to conduct reconnaissance efficiently. The choice of tools depends on the level of detail required and the engagement's scope.

1. Nmap (Network Mapper):
   - Purpose: A powerful tool for network discovery and security auditing.
   - Key Features:
     - Port scanning to identify open ports and services.
       - OS detection to determine the operating system running on a target.

- Scriptable interface using NSE (Nmap Scripting Engine) for advanced scanning.
- Use Case: Scanning a target network to identify open ports and running services that may have vulnerabilities.

2. Wireshark:

- Purpose: A network protocol analyzer used to capture and inspect network traffic in real-time.
- Key Features:
    - Captures packets for detailed inspection.
    - Filters traffic based on protocols, IP addresses, or ports.
    - Identifies unencrypted data, such as credentials transmitted in plain text.
    - Use Case: Monitoring a network to detect unusual traffic patterns or potential security breaches.

3. OSINT Techniques (Open Source Intelligence):

- Purpose: Leveraging publicly available information to gather intelligence about a target.
- Common Tools and Methods:
  - Shodan: A search engine for discovering internet-connected devices and services.
  - Maltego: A tool for visualizing relationships between entities such as IP addresses, domains, and individuals.
  - Google Dorking: Using advanced search queries to uncover sensitive information indexed by search engines.
  - Use Case: Identifying exposed credentials or unprotected systems by searching public data sources.

These tools provide comprehensive insights into the target's infrastructure, aiding ethical hackers in crafting their attack strategies.

Identifying Attack Surfaces

An attack surface is the total set of points where an attacker can attempt to gain unauthorized access to a system. Reducing the attack surface is a critical step in improving security posture.

1. Understanding Attack Surfaces:

- External Attack Surface: Includes internet-facing assets like web servers, APIs, and email servers.

- Internal Attack Surface: Comprises internal systems, applications, and networks accessible only to employees or trusted users.

- Human Attack Surface: Refers to the susceptibility of users to social engineering attacks, such as phishing.

2. Steps to Identify Attack Surfaces:

- Asset Inventory: Create a detailed inventory of all assets, including hardware, software, and data.

- Network Mapping: Use tools like Nmap or Zenmap to visualize the network structure and identify exposed nodes.

- Service Enumeration: Discover running services and applications using banner grabbing and port scanning.

- Vulnerability Scanning: Employ tools like Nessus or Qualys to detect known vulnerabilities in systems and applications.

3. Common Attack Surface Components:

- Web Applications: Often targeted for SQL injection, cross-site scripting (XSS), or remote code execution.

- APIs: Can be exploited if they lack proper authentication or input validation.

- IoT Devices: Frequently have weak security configurations and are vulnerable to attacks.

4. Minimizing the Attack Surface:

- Disable unused services and ports.

- Regularly update and patch software and hardware.

- Implement network segmentation to limit access to critical systems.

- Conduct regular penetration testing to uncover and address vulnerabilities.

Reconnaissance and information gathering are critical steps in ethical hacking, providing the necessary groundwork for identifying vulnerabilities and securing systems. By understanding the distinctions between passive and active reconnaissance, mastering tools like Nmap, Wireshark, and OSINT techniques, and thoroughly identifying attack surfaces, ethical hackers can ensure a comprehensive and ethical approach to penetration testing. This phase is not just about gathering data but doing so responsibly and within the boundaries of legality and professionalism.

Chapter 4: Scanning and Enumeration

Once reconnaissance is complete, the next step in ethical hacking is scanning and enumeration. These processes involve probing a target network or system to uncover vulnerabilities, live hosts, open ports, and running services. This chapter delves into network scanning techniques, the importance of enumeration, and the tools ethical hackers use, such as Nessus, Nikto, and netcat.

Network Scanning Techniques

Network scanning is a critical phase in penetration testing, enabling ethical hackers to identify weaknesses in a network's structure. Different scanning techniques are used depending on the level of stealth required and the information sought.

1. Ping Scans:

- Purpose: Determines which hosts are active on a network by sending ICMP (Internet Control Message Protocol) requests.
- Technique:
  - Tools like `ping` or `hping3` send echo requests to target IPs.
  - If a target responds, it is considered live.
  - Limitations: Firewalls or IDS/IPS systems often block ICMP traffic, making this method less reliable in secure environments.

2. Port Scanning:

- Purpose: Identifies open ports and associated services on a target host.
- Types of Port Scans:
  - TCP Connect Scan: Completes the three-way handshake to confirm an open port. It is accurate but easily detected.

- SYN Scan (Half-Open Scan): Sends a SYN packet but does not complete the handshake, making it stealthier.
- UDP Scan: Scans for open UDP ports, often used for discovering services like DNS or SNMP.
- Tools: Nmap is widely used for performing various port scanning techniques.

3. Stealth Scans:
- Purpose: Avoid detection by firewalls or IDS while scanning.
- Techniques:
- FIN Scan: Sends a FIN packet to the target. If no response is received, the port is likely open.
- Null Scan: Sends packets without any flags set, testing how the target responds.
- Xmas Scan: Sends a packet with all flags set.

4. Vulnerability Scanning:

- Purpose: Identifies known vulnerabilities in a system or network.
- Tools: Tools like Nessus and OpenVAS are used to detect misconfigurations, missing patches, and other security issues.

Identifying Live Hosts, Open Ports, and Services

Once a network scan is initiated, ethical hackers can start identifying critical elements for further exploitation.

1. Identifying Live Hosts:
- Use network discovery tools like Nmap or ARP scans to list active devices on a network.
- Example Command: `nmap -sn 192.168.1.0/24` (Performs a ping sweep to identify live hosts).

2. Identifying Open Ports:
- Open ports represent possible entry points into a system. Scanning tools like

Nmap can determine which ports are open and the services running on them.

- Example Command: `nmap -p- 192.168.1.100` (Scans all 65,535 ports on the target).

3. Enumerating Services:

- Banner Grabbing: Captures service banners to identify software versions and configurations.

- Example: Using netcat to grab a banner: `nc 192.168.1.100 80`

- Service version detection in Nmap: `nmap -sV 192.168.1.100`

- Identify running applications and match them against vulnerability databases to find potential weaknesses.

Tools for Scanning and Enumeration

The effectiveness of scanning and enumeration depends heavily on the tools used. Here are three essential tools for this phase:

1. Nessus:

- Overview: Nessus is a vulnerability scanner used to detect known vulnerabilities in systems, applications, and configurations.
- Key Features:
  - Scans for missing patches, misconfigurations, and weak passwords.
  - Generates detailed reports for remediation.
  - Integrates with compliance frameworks like PCI DSS and HIPAA.
- Use Case: An ethical hacker uses Nessus to scan a web server for vulnerabilities, identifying outdated software versions that require updates.

2. Nikto:

- Overview: Nikto is an open-source web server scanner that identifies vulnerabilities in web applications.
- Key Features:
  - Detects outdated software, insecure configurations, and common vulnerabilities.

- Scans for default credentials and admin interfaces.
- Comprehensive checks for more than 6,000 potential issues.
- Use Case: Scanning a target website with Nikto reveals a misconfigured web server leaking sensitive data.
- Example Command: `nikto -h http://192.168.1.100`

3. Netcat:
- Overview: Known as the "Swiss Army knife" of networking, netcat is used for port scanning, banner grabbing, and more.
- Key Features:
- Lightweight and versatile.
- Performs basic network connectivity tests.
- Used for creating simple backdoors during testing.
- Use Case: Using netcat to test connectivity to a target system's open port and retrieve the banner:

- Example Command: `nc -v 192.168.1.100 80`

Best Practices for Scanning and Enumeration

1. Adhere to Rules of Engagement (RoE):
- Ensure you have explicit permission before scanning any system.
- Define the scope of scanning to avoid accidental breaches.

2. Stealth and Timing:
- Use stealthy scanning techniques like SYN or FIN scans when necessary to avoid detection.
- Schedule scans during approved times to prevent disruption of normal operations.

3. Analyze Results Thoroughly:
- Cross-reference results with vulnerability databases like CVE

(Common Vulnerabilities and Exposures).
  - Validate findings manually to avoid false positives.

4. Document Findings:
  - Record all scanning activities, including tools, configurations, and results.
  - Provide detailed reports highlighting identified vulnerabilities and recommendations for remediation.

5. Use Multiple Tools:
  - Combine different tools to ensure comprehensive scanning and enumeration. For example, use Nmap for network scans and Nessus for vulnerability assessments.

Scanning and enumeration are fundamental stages of ethical hacking, providing detailed insights into a target's network and systems. By employing effective scanning techniques and leveraging tools like Nessus, Nikto, and netcat, ethical hackers can identify vulnerabilities and assess a system's security posture. Ethical considerations, thorough analysis, and detailed documentation ensure that this phase is conducted responsibly and professionally. These steps prepare hackers for the subsequent phases of penetration testing, where identified vulnerabilities can be exploited in a controlled and authorized manner.

Chapter 5: Exploitation and Gaining Access

Exploitation is the phase in ethical hacking where vulnerabilities discovered during earlier stages are leveraged to gain unauthorized access to systems, applications, or data. Ethical hackers simulate real-world attacks to identify the potential impact of exploitation, helping organizations address weaknesses and fortify their defenses. This chapter discusses the types of exploits, the use of Metasploit in penetration testing, and the process of writing and modifying simple exploits.

Exploit Types

Exploits are techniques or tools that take advantage of vulnerabilities in a target system to execute unauthorized actions. Ethical hackers categorize exploits based on how they interact with the system.

1. Remote Exploits:

- Definition: Exploits that target vulnerabilities in a system over a network without requiring direct access.
- Examples:
- Buffer Overflow Attacks: Exploiting improperly managed memory allocation to execute malicious code remotely.
- Remote Code Execution (RCE): Running arbitrary code on a target machine through vulnerable software or services.
- Use Case: Targeting a misconfigured FTP server to gain access without being physically present.

2. Local Exploits:

- Definition: Exploits that require an attacker to have some level of access to the system (e.g., as a user or via physical access).
- Examples:

- Privilege Escalation: Exploiting a flaw to increase access rights from a standard user to an administrator.
- Exploiting Weak Permissions: Gaining access to files or configurations that should be restricted.
- Use Case: An ethical hacker gains access to a system as a guest user and then escalates privileges to an admin using a kernel vulnerability.

3. Web Application Exploits:
- Definition: Exploits targeting vulnerabilities in web applications, APIs, or servers.
- Examples:
- SQL Injection (SQLi): Manipulating SQL queries to retrieve or modify sensitive database information.
- Cross-Site Scripting (XSS): Injecting malicious scripts into web pages viewed by users.
- File Inclusion Attacks: Exploiting improper file-handling logic to execute unintended code.

- Use Case: Exploiting an insecure web application to extract customer data from a backend database.

Using Metasploit for Penetration Testing

Metasploit is one of the most popular tools for penetration testing, offering a robust framework for exploiting vulnerabilities and gaining access to systems.

1. Overview of Metasploit Framework:
   - Purpose: A modular penetration testing framework used to develop, test, and execute exploits.
   - Components:
      - Exploits: Pre-built scripts targeting specific vulnerabilities.
      - Payloads: Code executed after a successful exploit to perform tasks like opening a reverse shell or installing malware.

- Auxiliary Modules: Tools for scanning, reconnaissance, and other non-exploit functions.

- Post-Exploitation Modules: Scripts for tasks like privilege escalation, keylogging, and data exfiltration.

2. Basic Workflow in Metasploit:
- Step 1: Start the Framework:
- Launch Metasploit using `msfconsole`.
- Step 2: Search for Exploits:
- Use `search` command to find exploits for specific vulnerabilities.
- Example: `search smb` (to find exploits for SMB vulnerabilities).
- Step 3: Configure the Exploit:
- Select an exploit using the `use` command.
- Example: `use exploit/windows/smb/ms17_010_etern alblue`.
- Step 4: Set Options:
- Configure target details like IP address or port using `set` commands.

- Example: `set RHOST 192.168.1.100`.

- Step 5: Select a Payload:

- Choose a payload that specifies the post-exploit action.

- Example: `set PAYLOAD windows/meterpreter/reverse_tcp`.

- Step 6: Run the Exploit:

- Launch the attack using `exploit` or `run`.

3. Common Scenarios Using Metasploit:

- Gaining Remote Access: Exploit a vulnerable service and deploy a reverse shell payload to gain remote control.

- Scanning and Reconnaissance: Use auxiliary modules for network scanning or banner grabbing.

- Automating Tasks: Use scripts to automate repetitive tasks, such as scanning multiple IP ranges for vulnerabilities.

Creating or modifying exploits is a critical skill for ethical hackers, helping them understand how vulnerabilities are exploited and how to mitigate them.

1. Understanding Exploits:

- Structure of an Exploit: Exploits typically include the following components:

- Trigger: Code that interacts with the vulnerability to cause unintended behavior.

- Payload Delivery: Mechanism for delivering the malicious code.

- Execution: Code that performs the intended action, such as opening a reverse shell.

2. Steps to Write a Simple Exploit:

- Step 1: Identify a Vulnerability:

- Use vulnerability databases like CVE or tools like Nessus to identify weaknesses.

- Step 2: Study the Target Application:
    - Analyze the application's source code or behavior to understand how the vulnerability can be triggered.
- Step 3: Craft Exploit Code:
    - Example (Python): Writing a basic buffer overflow exploit:
    ```python
    import socket

    target = "192.168.1.100"
    port = 8080
    payload = b"A" 1024  # Buffer overflow with 1024 'A's

    s = socket.socket(socket.AF_INET, socket.SOCK_STREAM)
    s.connect((target, port))
    s.send(payload)
    s.close()
    ```

- Step 4: Test the Exploit:
    - Use a virtual lab environment to test the exploit safely.

3. Modifying Existing Exploits:

- Locate Pre-built Exploits: Search exploit databases like Exploit-DB for scripts targeting specific vulnerabilities.
- Customize Code: Update exploit parameters, such as target IP addresses, ports, or payload types.
- Example: Modifying a Metasploit exploit to use a different payload:

```bash
set PAYLOAD linux/x86/meterpreter/reverse_tcp
```

4. Best Practices for Exploit Writing and Modification:

- Work in a Controlled Environment: Always test exploits in isolated environments to avoid accidental harm.
- Document Changes: Maintain detailed notes on modifications for reproducibility.
- Respect Legal Boundaries: Ensure exploit development aligns with legal and ethical guidelines.

The exploitation phase is a pivotal step in ethical hacking, enabling testers to demonstrate the real-world impact of vulnerabilities. Understanding the different types of exploits, leveraging tools like Metasploit, and developing custom exploits empowers ethical hackers to perform comprehensive penetration testing. By adhering to ethical guidelines and maintaining a focus on remediation, hackers can help organizations address critical weaknesses and improve their overall security posture.

Chapter 6: Privilege Escalation and Maintaining Access

Once an ethical hacker gains access to a system, the next objective is often to escalate privileges and secure persistent access. Privilege escalation involves leveraging vulnerabilities to gain higher levels of control within the system, such as administrator or root access. Maintaining access ensures continuity for further analysis or testing, while covering tracks is crucial for ethical hackers to simulate how malicious actors evade detection. This chapter explores techniques for privilege escalation, methods for persistence and obfuscation, and provides real-world examples to contextualize these activities.

Privilege escalation is typically categorized into vertical and horizontal escalation.

1. Vertical Privilege Escalation:
 - Involves moving from a lower-privileged account (e.g., user) to a higher-privileged account (e.g., admin or root).
  - Techniques:
   - Exploiting Kernel Vulnerabilities:
    - Using flaws in the operating system to execute privileged actions.
     - Example: Exploiting the Dirty COW vulnerability in Linux.
    - Weak Permissions on System Files:
     - Modifying or replacing executables that run with higher privileges.
      - Example: Writing malicious code into an executable in `/usr/bin`.
    - Password Exploitation:
     - Cracking or retrieving plaintext passwords for privileged accounts.

- Tools: John the Ripper, Hashcat.
- Privilege Misconfigurations:
    - Exploiting services running with excessive privileges (e.g., sudo misconfigurations).
    - Example: Abuse of the `sudo` command to execute arbitrary scripts.

2. Horizontal Privilege Escalation:
- Involves gaining access to other accounts with the same privilege level, often to expand reach or access sensitive data.
  - Techniques:
  - Credential Dumping:
    - Extracting stored passwords or hashes.
    - Tools: Mimikatz (Windows), LaZagne.
  - Session Hijacking:
    - Exploiting active user sessions to impersonate other users.
  - Tools: Ettercap, Cain & Abel.
  - Weak Password Policies:

- Using brute force or dictionary attacks to guess user credentials.

Once access is established, ethical hackers focus on ensuring they can maintain it without detection.

1. Covering Tracks:
  - Log Manipulation:
    - Deleting or modifying log files to remove evidence of activities.
      - Tools: PowerShell scripts (Windows), `sed` and `awk` (Linux).
  - File Timestamp Alteration:
    - Changing the creation, modification, or access timestamps of files to avoid suspicion.
      - Tools: `touch` command (Linux), timestomping utilities.
  - Process Hiding:
    - Concealing malicious processes to evade detection.

- Tools: Rootkits such as Azazel or Adore-ng.

2. Persistence Methods:
- Ensures that access can be regained after a system reboot or disconnection.
- Techniques:
  - Creating Backdoors:
    - Adding unauthorized access points.
    - Example: Deploying a reverse shell script that triggers on system startup.
  - Scheduled Tasks or Cron Jobs:
      - Automating malicious actions at regular intervals.
      - Example: Adding a cron job to execute a script that re-establishes a connection.
  - Registry Modifications (Windows):
      - Editing registry keys to load malicious programs on startup.
    - Tools: `regedit`, PowerShell.
  - Trojanized System Files:
      - Replacing legitimate system files with altered versions.

- Example: Modifying `/etc/passwd` to include a new privileged user.

Understanding practical applications of privilege escalation and persistence methods helps ethical hackers simulate real-world attack scenarios.

1. **Scenario 1: Exploiting Sudo Misconfigurations (Linux)**
    - Context: A non-root user account with limited privileges.
    - Exploit:
       - Checking sudo permissions: `sudo -l`.
          - Identifying an executable (`/usr/bin/nano`) that can run as root without a password.
          - Exploiting the executable to edit sensitive system files, such as `/etc/shadow`, to reset the root password.
    - Outcome: Privileged access achieved.

67

2. Scenario 2: Mimikatz for Credential Dumping (Windows)

- Context: A user has access to a Windows machine but needs admin credentials.
   - Exploit:
   - Using Mimikatz to dump credentials from memory:
   ```shell
   privilege::debug
   sekurlsa::logonpasswords
   ```

   - Extracting plaintext passwords or hashes for privileged accounts.
   - Outcome: Vertical escalation to administrator-level access.

3. Scenario 3: Persistence via Registry Modification (Windows)

- Context: Gained temporary access to a system but requires persistence.
   - Exploit:
   - Adding a malicious script to the `Run` key in the Windows registry:

```shell
reg add
HKCU\Software\Microsoft\Windows\CurrentVersion\Run /v backdoor /t REG_SZ /d "C:\malicious.exe"
```

- Outcome: The script executes automatically at each user login.

4. Scenario 4: Covering Tracks with Log Manipulation (Linux)

- Context: An ethical hacker executes a reverse shell but wants to erase logs.
- Exploit:
  - Accessing and editing log files:
  ```shell
  echo "" > /var/log/auth.log
  ```

- Outcome: Activity is no longer traceable in the logs.

Privilege escalation and maintaining access are critical stages in the ethical hacking process. These techniques help identify the potential damage an attacker could cause and ensure that vulnerabilities are mitigated effectively. By mastering escalation techniques, persistence methods, and track-covering strategies, ethical hackers can simulate advanced threats and provide valuable insights for improving organizational cybersecurity.

Chapter 7: Web Application Security

Web applications are a frequent target for attackers due to their accessibility over the internet and the sensitive data they often handle. Vulnerabilities in web applications can expose organizations to data breaches, fraud, and system compromises. Ethical hackers and penetration testers play a crucial role in identifying these vulnerabilities before malicious actors can exploit them. This chapter explores the most common web application vulnerabilities—SQL Injection, Cross-Site Scripting (XSS), and Cross-Site Request Forgery (CSRF)—providing hands-on examples with platforms like DVWA (Damn Vulnerable Web Application) and OWASP Juice Shop. Additionally, we discuss methods for securing web applications to mitigate these risks.

1. SQL Injection (SQLi):

SQL Injection occurs when an attacker manipulates a web application's database query by injecting malicious SQL code. This vulnerability can result in unauthorized access to the database, data exfiltration, or modification of sensitive information.

- How SQL Injection Works:
    - A typical web application that interacts with a database might use user input to generate SQL queries. If this input isn't properly sanitized, an attacker can manipulate the SQL query by injecting arbitrary commands.
    - Example: A vulnerable login form might generate a SQL query like:

```sql
SELECT FROM users WHERE username = 'user_input' AND password = 'user_input';
```

- If an attacker inputs `` `' OR '1'='1` ``, the query becomes:

```sql
SELECT FROM users WHERE username = '' OR '1'='1' AND password = '';
```

- This query will always return true, allowing the attacker to bypass authentication.

- Prevention Techniques:
- Prepared Statements/Parameterized Queries: These ensure that user input is treated as data, not code.
- Stored Procedures: Securely encapsulate database queries, separating data from logic.
- Input Validation and Sanitization: Validate user inputs using whitelisting and sanitize them to prevent harmful characters like single quotes (`` `'` ``) and semicolons (`` `;` ``).

2. Cross-Site Scripting (XSS):

Cross-Site Scripting involves injecting malicious scripts into web pages that are viewed by other users. XSS exploits trust in a website by allowing attackers to execute arbitrary scripts in the context of the victim's browser.

- How XSS Works:
    - In a vulnerable web application, user input such as comments, search queries, or user profiles may be reflected back into the web page without proper sanitization.
    - Example: A comment form may reflect the user's input directly onto a webpage without filtering HTML or JavaScript tags. If an attacker submits the following comment:
    ```html
    <script>alert('Hacked!');</script>
    ```

    - The script will execute in other users' browsers, displaying an alert box or worse, stealing session cookies or redirecting users to malicious sites.

- Prevention Techniques:
  - Input Encoding: Encode user input to ensure any HTML tags are rendered as text, not executable code.
    - Content Security Policy (CSP): Enforce policies that limit the sources from which scripts can be loaded.
  - Output Escaping: Escape potentially dangerous characters like `<`, `>`, `&`, and ``` in output.

3. Cross-Site Request Forgery (CSRF):

Cross-Site Request Forgery tricks the user's browser into performing an unwanted action on a trusted website where the user is authenticated. The attacker exploits the fact that browsers automatically include authentication credentials (like cookies) with each request.

- How CSRF Works:

- A typical CSRF attack involves embedding a malicious request (e.g., a form submission or image request) in a website that the victim visits while logged in to a target application.

- Example: If a user is logged into their banking application, an attacker could trick them into transferring money by embedding a request like this in an email or malicious webpage:

```html
<img src="https://bank.com/transfer?amount=1000&to=attacker_account" style="display:none;">
```

- When the victim's browser processes the request, it includes their session cookie, effectively transferring money without their consent.

- Prevention Techniques:
- Anti-CSRF Tokens: Generate and include unique tokens in every state-changing request (e.g., form

submissions), and verify them server-side.

- SameSite Cookies: Set the `SameSite` attribute on cookies to prevent them from being sent along with cross-site requests.

- Checking Referer Headers: Verify that requests are coming from trusted origins by inspecting the `Referer` header.

Hands-on Examples with DVWA and OWASP Juice Shop

1. DVWA (Damn Vulnerable Web Application):

DVWA is a platform specifically designed to practice web application security testing. It provides a variety of deliberately vulnerable web applications, allowing ethical hackers to practice exploiting common vulnerabilities like SQLi, XSS, and CSRF in a controlled environment.

- Setting Up DVWA:

1. Download and install DVWA on a local server (e.g., XAMPP or LAMP).

2. Access the DVWA interface in a web browser.

3. Adjust the security level (low, medium, high) based on your testing requirements.

- Testing SQL Injection with DVWA:

- Navigate to the "SQL Injection" section and try injecting SQL payloads into user input fields (e.g., login forms).

- Example: Try `admin' OR '1'='1` as the username and password to bypass authentication.

- Testing XSS with DVWA:

- Navigate to the "XSS (Reflected)" section and input a simple script in the user comment field:

```html
<script>alert('XSS');</script>
```

- Observe whether the script executes in the browser of another user viewing the page.

- Testing CSRF with DVWA:
- Navigate to the CSRF section, and attempt to perform a CSRF attack by crafting a malicious request using an HTML form that will change the user's password or perform another action without their consent.

2. OWASP Juice Shop:

OWASP Juice Shop is an intentionally insecure web application that simulates a modern e-commerce platform. It is a great platform for learning and practicing various web security vulnerabilities, including SQLi, XSS, and CSRF.

- Setting Up OWASP Juice Shop:
1. Clone the Juice Shop repository from GitHub or use the Docker version to quickly deploy it.

2. Start the application and access it in a web browser.

3. Engage with the application and attempt to identify vulnerabilities in different parts of the app.

- Testing SQL Injection with Juice Shop:
    - Attempt to manipulate the login form by entering SQL payloads into the username and password fields.
    - Observe the database query errors or unexpected behavior that might indicate a vulnerability.

- Testing XSS with Juice Shop:
    - Explore input fields, such as the search box or product review form. Inject various XSS payloads and see if the application reflects unfiltered input in the page's output.

- Testing CSRF with Juice Shop:

- Craft a CSRF attack by creating a hidden form or image that submits requests on behalf of a logged-in user.
- Verify whether the application properly validates the origin of requests and implements anti-CSRF protections.

Securing Web Applications

Securing web applications is essential to protecting them from common vulnerabilities. The following strategies are key for building secure applications:

1. Input Validation and Output Encoding:
- Implement strict input validation, allowing only safe characters and rejecting harmful inputs.
- Use output encoding to ensure user input is never treated as executable code.

2. Use of HTTPS:

- Encrypt data in transit by enforcing HTTPS for all communication between the client and server. This protects against eavesdropping and man-in-the-middle attacks.

3. Session Management:
- Implement secure session handling practices, including using secure, HttpOnly, and SameSite cookies.
- Ensure sessions expire after a reasonable period of inactivity.

4. Regular Security Audits:
- Conduct regular security assessments, including penetration testing, code reviews, and vulnerability scans.
- Use automated tools like OWASP ZAP and Burp Suite to identify security flaws.

5. Security Headers:
- Implement HTTP security headers like Content-Security-Policy (CSP),

X-Content-Type-Options, and X-XSS-Protection to reduce attack surface.

- Disable unnecessary HTTP methods such as `TRACE` and `OPTIONS`.

Web application security is a fundamental aspect of cybersecurity, as vulnerabilities in web applications can expose sensitive data and compromise system integrity. By understanding common vulnerabilities such as SQLi, XSS, and CSRF, ethical hackers can better defend applications through proactive testing and remediation. Hands-on platforms like DVWA and OWASP Juice Shop offer valuable learning environments, enabling security professionals to apply their knowledge in real-world scenarios. Finally, securing web applications requires a multi-layered approach, incorporating best practices in input validation, session management, and regular security audits to reduce the risk of attacks.

Chapter 8: Wireless Network Penetration Testing

Wireless networks have become ubiquitous in both personal and organizational settings, offering convenience and flexibility. However, their inherent vulnerabilities make them prime targets for attackers. Wireless network penetration testing involves assessing the security of wireless networks to identify potential vulnerabilities and weaknesses. Ethical hackers play a crucial role in performing these tests, ensuring that weaknesses are addressed before malicious actors can exploit them. This chapter provides an in-depth understanding of wireless network penetration testing, focusing on breaking WEP/WPA encryption, using essential tools such as Aircrack-ng and Kismet, and addressing the ethical concerns that arise during wireless network testing.

1. WEP (Wired Equivalent Privacy):

WEP was once a widely used encryption standard for wireless networks, but it is now considered outdated and insecure. WEP is vulnerable to several attacks, most notably due to its use of weak initialization vectors (IVs) and static encryption keys.

- Weaknesses in WEP:
  - Weak IVs: WEP uses a 24-bit IV, which is relatively short and leads to IV reuse, making it easier for attackers to perform statistical analysis and recover the encryption key.
  - RC4 Algorithm Weaknesses: The RC4 cipher, which WEP uses for encryption, is flawed, and attackers can exploit these flaws to recover plaintext data.

- Shared Key Authentication Vulnerabilities: The process of shared key authentication can also be exploited to crack the WEP key.

- WEP Cracking Process:
To crack WEP, attackers typically perform the following steps:

1. Packet Sniffing: Use a wireless network sniffer, such as Kismet or Wireshark, to capture a large number of data packets transmitted over the network.

2. Collecting IVs: The attacker looks for repeated IVs, which are crucial for cracking the WEP key. The more IVs collected, the higher the chances of successfully cracking the encryption.

3. Key Recovery: Once enough IVs are captured, tools like Aircrack-ng can be used to apply statistical techniques to recover the WEP encryption key. This process is highly dependent on the number of packets and IVs captured.

- Cracking Tools:

- Aircrack-ng: Aircrack-ng is a powerful suite of tools used for assessing the security of wireless networks. It can be used to capture packets, inject packets into the network, and crack WEP and WPA encryption. The tool's primary function in WEP cracking is to perform statistical analysis on captured packets and break the encryption key.

- Kismet: Kismet is a wireless network detector, sniffer, and intrusion detection system. It allows attackers to discover hidden wireless networks and capture packets from networks running WEP encryption. Kismet is a useful tool for identifying weak IVs and obtaining the data required to crack WEP keys.

2. WPA (Wi-Fi Protected Access):

WPA was introduced as a more secure alternative to WEP, addressing many of the vulnerabilities inherent in WEP. WPA uses the TKIP (Temporal Key Integrity Protocol) encryption protocol, which provides dynamic encryption keys, making it harder to crack than WEP.

- WPA2:

WPA2 is the successor to WPA and is considered much more secure. WPA2 uses the AES (Advanced Encryption Standard) protocol, which is significantly stronger than TKIP. However, WPA2 is still vulnerable to certain attacks, such as the PMKID (Pairwise Master Key Identifier) attack, which targets the handshake process in WPA2 authentication.

- Breaking WPA/WPA2 Encryption:
  - Capturing the WPA Handshake: WPA/WPA2 networks use a four-way handshake to authenticate clients to the access point. An attacker can capture this handshake by listening to network traffic when a client connects to the access point.

- Brute Force Attacks: Once the handshake is captured, the attacker can attempt to crack the WPA key using brute force or dictionary attacks. Tools like Aircrack-ng can be used to perform these attacks by testing potential passphrases against the captured handshake.

- PMKID Attack: In WPA2, attackers can capture the PMKID by forcing the client and access point to exchange certain packets. The PMKID is part of the WPA2 handshake, and attackers can use it to perform an offline brute-force attack, bypassing the need to wait for a client to connect.

- Tools for Cracking WPA/WPA2:

- Aircrack-ng: Aircrack-ng can be used for WPA and WPA2 attacks, particularly for capturing handshakes and performing offline brute-force attacks against the captured hash.

- Hashcat: Hashcat is a popular password-cracking tool that can be used in conjunction with Aircrack-ng to perform high-speed brute-force attacks on WPA handshakes.

- Reaver: Reaver is a tool designed to attack WPS (Wi-Fi Protected Setup) PINs, which are used for simplifying WPA/WPA2 authentication. WPS has a known vulnerability where the PIN is only 8 digits long, making it susceptible to brute-force attacks.

Tools: Aircrack-ng, Kismet, and Others

1. Aircrack-ng:

Aircrack-ng is one of the most widely used tools for wireless network penetration testing. It is a suite of tools that can be used for packet sniffing, injection, and cracking wireless network encryption. The key functionalities of Aircrack-ng include:

- Packet Capture: Aircrack-ng allows you to capture packets from a target wireless network to collect the necessary data for cracking encryption.

- WEP/WPA Cracking: It can crack WEP and WPA encryption by analyzing the captured packets and performing dictionary or brute-force attacks.

- Injection: Aircrack-ng can inject packets into the network to accelerate the process of capturing the necessary data, such as obtaining IVs for WEP or triggering the WPA handshake.

2. Kismet:

Kismet is a powerful wireless network detector and sniffer. It allows ethical hackers to passively monitor wireless networks, detect hidden SSIDs, and capture network traffic for further analysis. Key features of Kismet include:

- Network Detection: Kismet can discover hidden wireless networks by analyzing the beacons broadcast by access points.

- Packet Capture: It can capture packets on different channels, making it useful for identifying weak IVs in WEP-encrypted networks.

- Sniffing Multiple Networks: Kismet supports sniffing multiple networks at once, allowing for large-scale wireless network analysis.

3. Other Tools:
- Reaver: As mentioned earlier, Reaver is a tool designed for exploiting vulnerabilities in WPS to obtain the WPA/WPA2 key.
- Wireshark: While primarily known as a network protocol analyzer, Wireshark can also be used for wireless network analysis. It allows testers to capture and analyze packets on both wired and wireless networks.

Ethical Concerns in Wireless Testing

Ethical hacking, including wireless network penetration testing, requires strict adherence to legal and ethical guidelines to avoid causing harm to individuals, organizations, or systems.

The following ethical concerns should be carefully considered:

1. Authorization and Consent:

Always obtain explicit permission before performing penetration testing on any wireless network. Testing a network without authorization is illegal and can result in criminal charges. This applies to both personal and corporate networks. Unauthorized access to any network is considered hacking, regardless of intent.

2. Privacy and Confidentiality:

Wireless network penetration testing may involve the interception of sensitive data, including personal or corporate information. Ethical hackers must respect the privacy of individuals and organizations by ensuring that any data intercepted during testing is not misused. Confidentiality agreements should be signed to ensure that any sensitive information encountered during testing is not disclosed.

3. Non-Disruptive Testing:

Penetration testers must ensure that their activities do not disrupt or damage the target network. For example, cracking WEP or WPA encryption could potentially cause the access point to disconnect legitimate users, leading to a denial-of-service (DoS) condition. Ethical hackers should conduct testing in a controlled manner to minimize disruptions.

4. Responsibility and Reporting:

Once vulnerabilities are discovered during a wireless network penetration test, the tester must report them to the organization promptly and responsibly. Ethical hackers should provide actionable recommendations to remediate the vulnerabilities and offer guidance on securing the network.

5. Compliance with Laws and Regulations:

Ethical hackers must be aware of local, regional, and international laws regarding hacking and cybersecurity. Laws vary widely, and ethical hackers should always operate within the boundaries of the law. Additionally, compliance with regulations such as GDPR (General Data Protection Regulation) and HIPAA (Health Insurance Portability and Accountability Act) should be ensured when testing networks handling sensitive data.

Wireless network penetration testing is an essential part of cybersecurity, allowing organizations to identify and mitigate vulnerabilities in their wireless infrastructure. By understanding how to break WEP/WPA encryption, using tools like Aircrack-ng and Kismet, and adhering to ethical principles, ethical hackers can help secure wireless networks and prevent attacks. However, it is crucial to approach wireless network testing with a clear understanding of the legal, ethical, and technical considerations involved to ensure that testing is conducted responsibly and in compliance with the law.

Chapter 9: Reporting and Remediation

In ethical hacking, penetration testing is only one part of the process. The real value comes from how vulnerabilities are communicated and addressed after testing is complete. Writing clear, professional reports, providing actionable remediation steps, and emphasizing the importance of continuous monitoring are key to ensuring that the vulnerabilities discovered during testing are properly mitigated. This chapter focuses on the essential steps involved in reporting findings and creating a remediation plan to help organizations enhance their security posture.

Writing Professional Penetration Testing Reports

A penetration testing report is the primary deliverable after an assessment is completed. It serves as both a detailed account of the testing process and a guide for the organization to mitigate discovered vulnerabilities. A well-structured report should be comprehensive, clear, and actionable. Below are the key components of a professional penetration testing report:

1. Executive Summary

- Purpose: The executive summary provides a high-level overview of the penetration test's goals, scope, and results. It is intended for senior management or non-technical stakeholders who need to understand the key findings without diving into technical details.

- Content: It should briefly explain the objectives of the test, the methodologies used, and an overview of the discovered vulnerabilities. The executive summary should include a risk assessment, emphasizing the critical issues that need immediate attention.

- Tone: Keep the tone clear and concise. Avoid overly technical jargon, and focus on the business impact of vulnerabilities, such as the potential financial and reputational damage if they remain unaddressed.

2. Scope of the Test
- Description of the Test Scope: This section outlines the boundaries of the test—what was tested and what was excluded. This may include specific systems, networks, applications, or physical locations that were tested. It is crucial to clarify whether the test was conducted on the entire infrastructure or a subset of systems.

- Objectives: Clearly state the objectives of the test, such as identifying vulnerabilities, exploiting them to gain unauthorized access, or evaluating the strength of defense mechanisms. A well-defined scope ensures there is no ambiguity in the final report.

3. Methodology
 - Testing Approach: Detail the approach and tools used during the penetration test. Describe the stages of testing, such as information gathering, scanning, enumeration, exploitation, and post-exploitation.
 - Tools and Techniques: Include a list of the tools (e.g., Metasploit, Nmap, Burp Suite) and techniques used to conduct the test. This section demonstrates the thoroughness and professionalism of the testing process.
 - Types of Tests: Indicate if the test was black-box (no prior knowledge), white-box (full knowledge), or gray-box (limited knowledge) testing. Each approach may influence the findings and depth of the report.

4. Detailed Findings and Vulnerabilities
 - Identified Vulnerabilities: This section is the core of the report, where vulnerabilities discovered during the

testing process are listed and described in detail. For each vulnerability, include the following information:

   - Description: A clear and concise explanation of the vulnerability, including how it was discovered and the impact it could have on the system.

   - Risk Level: Assign a severity rating to each vulnerability (e.g., Critical, High, Medium, Low). This helps prioritize remediation efforts.

   - Evidence: Provide evidence of the vulnerability, such as screenshots, logs, or proof-of-concept exploits.

   - CVE (Common Vulnerabilities and Exposures) Reference: If applicable, reference any publicly known vulnerabilities (e.g., CVE IDs) associated with the findings.

   - Example:
      - Vulnerability: SQL Injection in Login Page
      - Risk Level: High

- Evidence: Screenshots of SQL injection payloads executed on the login form, revealing unauthorized access to the database.

- Impact: Attackers can gain access to sensitive user data, modify records, or even delete information. This could lead to data breaches and loss of customer trust.

5. Remediation Recommendations

For each vulnerability, offer practical and actionable remediation steps to resolve the issues. These steps should be clear, specific, and feasible. Suggestions may include:

- Patch Management: Updating software to fix known vulnerabilities (e.g., applying security patches).

- Configuration Changes: Recommending configuration changes to tighten security, such as disabling unnecessary services or enforcing stronger password policies.

- Code Fixes: Offering advice on securing applications, like using parameterized queries to prevent SQL injection or implementing input validation to avoid Cross-Site Scripting (XSS).

- Security Tools: Recommending specific security tools (e.g., Web Application Firewalls, Anti-virus software) that could mitigate future attacks.

6. Conclusion and Next Steps

- Summary of Findings: Summarize the most critical vulnerabilities and provide a brief recap of the remediation recommendations.

- Next Steps: Outline the recommended follow-up actions, including patching vulnerabilities, enhancing security measures, or scheduling future assessments. Stress the importance of implementing fixes in a timely manner to reduce the risk of exploitation.

Communicating Vulnerabilities and Remediation Steps

Effective communication of vulnerabilities and remediation steps is crucial for ensuring that the necessary actions are taken. When communicating findings to both technical and non-technical audiences, the following considerations should be kept in mind:

1. Technical Communication:
For security professionals, system administrators, and developers, the focus should be on the technical aspects of the vulnerabilities. Use precise, technical language and provide in-depth details about how the vulnerabilities can be exploited and mitigated.

- Clear Technical Details: Provide step-by-step guides to reproduce the issue and potential attack scenarios. Use clear diagrams, flowcharts, or code snippets to explain the vulnerabilities and suggested fixes.

- Tools and References: List any tools or frameworks used to discover the vulnerabilities and recommend specific security tools for remediation. Provide links to public resources, such as CVE databases or technical blogs, for further reading.

2. Non-Technical Communication:

When communicating with management or non-technical stakeholders, focus on the business impact and potential risks of the vulnerabilities. Avoid overly complex technical language and instead focus on how vulnerabilities could affect the company's reputation, data integrity, financial stability, and customer trust.

- Business Risks: Frame each vulnerability in terms of the potential consequences (e.g., data breaches, downtime, legal issues).
- Actionable Steps: Provide a roadmap for remediation that includes prioritizing the most critical

vulnerabilities first and providing timelines for implementing fixes.

3. Collaboration:

Penetration testers should work closely with the development and security teams during the remediation process to ensure that fixes are properly implemented. Collaboration is key in identifying any roadblocks, testing fixes, and ensuring that vulnerabilities are thoroughly resolved.

The Importance of Continuous Monitoring

Penetration testing provides a snapshot of an organization's security posture at a particular point in time, but it is only part of an ongoing security strategy. Continuous monitoring is essential to maintain long-term security and ensure that vulnerabilities do not reappear or new threats do not emerge.

1. Evolving Threat Landscape:

The cybersecurity landscape is constantly changing, with new threats and vulnerabilities emerging regularly. Attackers are always looking for new ways to exploit weaknesses, which means that organizations must stay vigilant. Continuous monitoring helps detect and respond to threats in real-time, minimizing the window of opportunity for attackers.

2. Proactive Detection:

Continuous monitoring allows organizations to identify potential vulnerabilities before they are exploited. Security Information and Event Management (SIEM) systems, intrusion detection systems (IDS), and network monitoring tools can provide real-time alerts on unusual activity, helping organizations take immediate action.

- Real-Time Alerts: SIEM systems aggregate logs from various sources and analyze them for signs of malicious behavior.

- Automated Responses: Many monitoring tools can trigger automated responses to mitigate attacks, such as blocking IP addresses or isolating compromised systems.

3. Improving the Security Posture:

Regular penetration tests followed by continuous monitoring provide valuable feedback loops for improving security practices. Penetration testing reveals the effectiveness of existing controls, and continuous monitoring ensures that systems remain secure over time. Regular vulnerability scans, patching, and updating are necessary to keep security up to date.

4. Compliance and Risk Management:

For many organizations, continuous monitoring is a requirement for regulatory compliance (e.g., HIPAA,

GDPR). Maintaining an active security posture and documenting findings and responses ensures that the organization meets the necessary compliance standards and avoids legal liabilities.

5. Security Awareness:

Continuous monitoring can also help enhance an organization's security awareness culture. By regularly reviewing security logs and alerts, organizations can better understand the types of threats they face and refine their response strategies.

Reporting and remediation are critical components of the penetration testing process. Writing clear, professional reports and communicating vulnerabilities and remediation steps effectively are key to ensuring that security issues are addressed. Additionally, continuous monitoring is essential for maintaining security in the long run. Organizations must not only act on the findings from penetration tests but also establish systems for ongoing vigilance and response to new threats. This holistic approach ensures a proactive security strategy and minimizes the risk of exploitation in the future.

Chapter 10: Career Path and Further Learning

In the rapidly evolving world of cybersecurity, ethical hacking presents a unique and exciting career path. As the number of cyber threats grows, the demand for skilled ethical hackers continues to rise. However, the journey in ethical hacking is not a destination but a continuous learning process. This chapter will explore the various career opportunities in ethical hacking, the importance of certifications and advanced courses, how to stay updated on trends and emerging threats, and the role of community engagement in shaping a successful career.

Certifications and Advanced Courses

Ethical hackers need to build a solid foundation of technical knowledge and practical skills. One of the most effective ways to gain credibility and demonstrate competence is by earning recognized certifications. These certifications not only validate skills but also help individuals advance in their careers. Additionally, as technology and threats evolve, pursuing advanced courses and specializations is essential for staying competitive in the field.

1. Certified Ethical Hacker (CEH)

- The CEH certification, offered by EC-Council, is one of the most widely recognized certifications in ethical hacking. It provides foundational knowledge about ethical hacking tools and techniques, including network scanning, penetration testing, and system exploitation.

- Requirements: To become CEH certified, candidates typically need two years of work experience in the Information Security domain or must take an official EC-Council training course.

- Scope: This certification covers topics such as penetration testing, vulnerability analysis, cryptography, and web application security. It provides a comprehensive overview of the ethical hacking process, making it suitable for those new to the field or looking to formalize their existing knowledge.

2. Offensive Security Certified Professional (OSCP)

- The OSCP, offered by Offensive Security, is known for its hands-on approach to ethical hacking. It is considered one of the most challenging and respected certifications in the industry. OSCP certifies penetration testers in real-world, practical skills and emphasizes the ability to exploit vulnerabilities and gain access to systems.

- Requirements: Candidates must complete the Offensive Security's Penetration Testing with Kali Linux

(PWK) course, which includes training and practical labs.

- Scope: The OSCP exam requires candidates to perform an actual penetration test in a controlled environment, where they must identify vulnerabilities, exploit them, and provide a comprehensive report. The focus is on hands-on, real-world skills and not just theoretical knowledge.

3. Certified Information Systems Security Professional (CISSP)

- The CISSP certification, offered by ISC2, is geared towards experienced professionals who wish to deepen their understanding of security management, governance, and risk management. While not specifically focused on ethical hacking, it is an important certification for those seeking to move into higher-level security roles or managerial positions.

- Requirements: To earn the CISSP, candidates need five years of experience in at least two of the eight domains of information security.

- Scope: This certification covers a broad range of topics, including access control, security architecture, cryptography, and security operations.

4. Certified Cloud Security Professional (CCSP)

- With the rise of cloud computing, the CCSP certification (also offered by ISC2) has become increasingly relevant. It focuses on cloud security best practices, including securing cloud environments, managing cloud risks, and understanding cloud compliance requirements.

- Requirements: Candidates must have a minimum of five years of work experience in information technology, with at least three years in information security and one year in cloud security.

- Scope: The CCSP certification covers cloud architecture, governance, compliance, and risk management, making it ideal for ethical hackers involved in cloud security testing.

5. Advanced and Specialized Courses

- Penetration Testing & Vulnerability Assessment: As attackers use increasingly sophisticated methods, professionals must have a deep understanding of vulnerabilities and exploitation techniques. Advanced penetration testing courses, often provided by platforms like Udemy, Coursera, or SANS Institute, cover specialized topics like advanced web application testing, wireless security, and exploit development.

- Malware Analysis & Reverse Engineering: Malware analysis is another area where specialized skills are in demand. Professionals can take courses in reverse engineering, learning how to disassemble malicious code, understand its behavior, and develop defenses against it.

- Digital Forensics: Understanding how digital forensics works, including evidence collection, chain of custody, and forensic analysis tools, is valuable for ethical hackers involved in incident response.

Cybersecurity is an ever-changing landscape. New vulnerabilities, attack vectors, and exploits are discovered daily, making it essential for ethical hackers to stay current. Continuous learning is key to remaining effective in identifying and mitigating evolving threats.

1. Follow Cybersecurity Blogs and Websites
- Security Research Blogs: Some well-known cybersecurity blogs, such as Krebs on Security, The Hacker News, and Dark Reading, provide in-depth coverage of the latest security threats,

vulnerabilities, and hacking techniques. These blogs also offer insights into cybersecurity trends and the latest research in ethical hacking.

- Tool and Exploit News: Websites such as Exploit-DB and Packet Storm provide up-to-date information on newly discovered exploits, tools, and techniques. These sources are invaluable for ethical hackers looking to stay informed about emerging threats and tools.

2. Follow Cybersecurity Conferences

- Black Hat and DEF CON: These two conferences are among the most prominent in the cybersecurity industry. They feature presentations, workshops, and demonstrations on the latest threats, hacking techniques, and security research. Attending such conferences can provide an opportunity to network with industry professionals and learn about cutting-edge techniques.

 - OWASP AppSec and RSA Conference: OWASP (Open Web Application Security Project) focuses on application security, and its AppSec conferences are a great resource for web application security professionals. The RSA Conference brings together experts in all aspects of cybersecurity and is a valuable resource for ethical hackers to gain insights into the latest trends and best practices.

3. Podcasts and YouTube Channels

 - Podcasts like Security Now, Darknet Diaries, and The CyberWire offer regular discussions about current threats and cybersecurity news.

 - YouTube channels such as IppSec, LiveOverflow, and The Cyber Mentor provide hands-on demonstrations of penetration testing and ethical hacking techniques. These channels offer great tutorials, walkthroughs of hacking challenges, and explanations of security concepts.

4. Threat Intelligence Platforms

- Open-Source Threat Intelligence (OSINT): Ethical hackers should familiarize themselves with open-source threat intelligence tools like MISP (Malware Information Sharing Platform) and CIRCL (Computer Incident Response Center Luxembourg). These platforms aggregate and share threat data, including indicators of compromise (IoC), which can help ethical hackers understand and defend against emerging threats.

- Commercial Threat Intelligence Providers: Subscribing to commercial threat intelligence services such as FireEye, Palo Alto Networks, or CrowdStrike can also provide real-time updates on cyber threats, vulnerabilities, and the tactics used by malicious actors.

Community and Resources (e.g., Bug Bounty Platforms)

The cybersecurity community plays an essential role in the ongoing development of ethical hacking skills. Being part of a community provides opportunities for learning, collaboration, and growth. Furthermore, participation in programs like bug bounty platforms can offer practical experience and even monetary rewards for discovering vulnerabilities.

1. Bug Bounty Platforms

- HackerOne: HackerOne is one of the most popular bug bounty platforms where ethical hackers can find vulnerabilities in real-world applications and systems. Many large organizations, such as Uber, Facebook, and GitHub, run bug bounty programs on HackerOne.

- Bugcrowd: Bugcrowd is another well-known bug bounty platform offering various programs for penetration testers to discover vulnerabilities and report them for rewards. Participating in these programs allows ethical hackers to gain real-world experience while contributing to improving security.

- Synack: Synack offers a private bug bounty platform where testers are vetted before being given access to specific programs. The platform focuses on helping businesses strengthen their security by leveraging the skills of ethical hackers.

2. Online Communities and Forums

- Reddit (r/Netsec, r/AskNetsec): Reddit's cybersecurity communities are great places to stay updated on the latest news, trends, and best practices. They also provide opportunities to ask questions, share knowledge, and network with other security professionals.

- Stack Exchange (Information Security): Stack Exchange's Information Security community is a Q&A platform where ethical hackers and security professionals exchange advice, tips, and troubleshooting techniques.

3. Meetups and Hackathons
- Attending local meetups or participating in cybersecurity hackathons can provide hands-on practice and networking opportunities. Many cities host regular events where ethical hackers can meet other professionals, share experiences, and learn about new tools and techniques.

4. Capture The Flag (CTF) Competitions
- Hack The Box (HTB): HTB offers a platform for ethical hackers to solve various penetration testing challenges in a virtual environment. The platform has a variety of difficulty levels, making it

suitable for both beginners and experienced professionals.

- CTFtime: CTFtime is a website that tracks the best Capture The Flag (CTF) competitions. Participating in CTFs is a great way to practice penetration testing skills and challenge yourself in a competitive environment.

Ethical hacking is a dynamic and rewarding career that requires continuous learning and adaptation to stay ahead of ever-evolving cyber threats. Certifications, advanced courses, and staying updated on the latest trends and threats are essential for progressing in the field. Additionally, engaging with the cybersecurity community, contributing to bug bounty programs, and participating

In CTF competitions offer invaluable opportunities for growth. By dedicating yourself to learning, networking, and honing your practical skills, you can build a successful and fulfilling career as an ethical hacker.

www.ingramcontent.com/pod-product-compliance
Lightning Source LLC
LaVergne TN
LVHW022351060326
832902LV00022B/4382